# WHAT IS STUPID?

**S**urely we've all asked ourselves this question at one time or another. To some *Gilligan's Island* is quintessential stupidity. Certain politicians have earned the right to be called stupid. Stupid is the way many of us act on our first date. In all fairness, it is safe to say that each of us has our own exquisite hour in the spotlight of stupidity sometime during our lives.

With Herculean endurance, the authors of this book have worked to uncover the stupidest of bar tricks. Our dangerous task took us to nightspots throughout the world, many of which were of the most questionable nature.

Here, presented for your enjoyment, is a compilation of some of the stupidest bar tricks known to man.

10 9 8 7 6 5 4 3 2 1
The digit on the right indicates the number of this printing

Library of Congress Cataloging-in-Publication Data
Steinfeld, Adam, 1958-
    Adam Steinfeld's stupid bar tricks.
    Rev. ed. of: Stupid bar tricks. c1986.
    1. Tricks. 2. Drinking games. I. McCormick, Bret.
    II. Title. III. Title: Stupid bar tricks.
GV 1559.S74   1993   793.2   87-43260
ISBN 0-939639-02-5

Grateful acknowledgment is made to Dal Sanders and Lou Simmons for permission to quote from their song: "A Girl Like You" ©1986 Cricket Hollow Music. All rights reserved. Used by permission.

Illustrations by Benjamin Vincent and Vincent Waller

Front cover illustration by Benjamin Vincent

Book design: Adam Steinfeld

This book may be ordered by mail from the publisher.
    Now That's Funny! Publishing
    P.O. Box 15788
    Ft. Lauderdale, FL 33318

    $5.95 per copy + $2.50 S&H

Adam Steinfeld's stupid bar tricks.
Rev. ed. of: Stupid bar tricks. ©1986.
1. Tricks. 2. Drinking games. I. McCormick, Bret.

*Adam Steinfeld's*

# *STUPID*

# *BAR*

# *TRICKS*

### *ADAM STEINFELD*

### *BRET McCORMICK*

*NOW THAT'S FUNNY! PUBLISHING*
*FT. LAUDERDALE, FLORIDA*

This book is dedicated to Sarah & Lisa,
the Supreme Goddesses of Love & Stupidity...
Friends forever!

# Acknowledgments

It's easy to write and give the plaudits and accolades of people who helped elevate this book to the highest level possible.

*Stupid Bar Tricks* might have remained a simplistic trick book but these creative people would never let it happen. To everyone whom I talked with about the concept and felt it was a strong idea - Thank you -

Special Thanks to:

Bret McCormick, your humorous writings added a true sense of the word comedy which fostered this end result. Also thanks to Carolyn McCormick for picture posing.

Benjamin Vincent for illustrating and transforming a mild-mannered comedy book into a truly superbook. Also to Vincent Waller for creating the beginning illustrations which gave the characters life.

Larry Ford for doing a superior graphic layout giving the book form, reality and polish.

Dal Sanders, my friend and fellow magician, for the contribution of his song, "A Girl Like You" and his bar trick, "My Palm Line," who first talked with Dubonnet about my manuscript.

Craig Meier and Richard Chapman who believed in the idea enough to start the presses rolling.

All the bartenders and bar friends I have met throughout my lifetime, who can always remember the fool who showed them a Stupid Bar Trick.

-A.B.S.-

# Adam Steinfeld's
# STUPID BAR TRICKS

written

by

**Adam Steinfeld**

&

Bret McCormick

illustrations

**Benjamin Vincent**

&

**Vincent Waller**

graphic layout

**Larry Ford**

# NOW THAT'S FUNNY! PUBLISHING
# FT. LAUDERDALE, FLORIDA

# CONTENTS

# *FOREWORD*

I don't believe it! That's impossible! How did he do it? As the masses of people utter these words of disbelief, remember the originator of stupidity. That is STUPID BAR TRICKS.

Do I seem like I'm rambling? Well maybe it's because magician Adam Steinfeld is truly a genius when it comes to bar tricks. He's an invader of logic, a tour de force of STUPIDUS. What's that? Well I'll tell ya.

Adam Steinfeld performs skillful manipulative magic in discos, nightclubs and even the corner bar. Legend has it one night ... Hey what is this? The origin of Superman or something? No, now wait a minute ...

One evening Adam was entertaining at a nightclub showing tricks at many of the tables, when a Marilyn Monroe type was watching him with much enthusiasm. His tricks could do no wrong; her eyes lit up with tremendous delight as he entertained.

Well, at that moment a jealous bartender attempted to show the blond beauty a bar trick to win her over. Her eyes turned on the bartender performing a really simplistic presentation. He was balancing a glass on top of a dollar bill over two glasses. "That's STUPID," yelled Adam.

I've never seen anything like it. It was a battle of the magicians. Adam became less and less patient with the bartender's performance. Standing across the dance floor, he picked up a coaster and threw it seventy-five feet across the room. It came to a stop knocking down the two glasses.

Everyone cheered him on in triumph. They crowned him the winner and he escorted the lovely lady home. Established as the new champion Adam was given the title of the master of STUPID BAR TRICKS. It was a great moment in bar history and I'm glad I was a witness.

I heard later he vowed to share with the world many of his secrets of Stupidity. Rumor has it that he met up with a writer named Bret McCormick who writes and lives horror and comedy.

After much research, they scribbled out on paper the doctrines of the Stupidity of Bar Tricks. Soon everyone will be a part of the world of Stupid Bar Tricks and share in the ancient philosophy of Stupidity.

-A.B.S.-

# 1
## Finger Stretch

I f you want to perform an impressive bar trick which will astound your companions then skip over this one. However, if you are too intoxicated to execute any of the other tricks in this book, by all means proceed.

# *Finger Stretch*

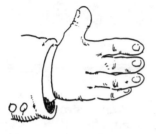

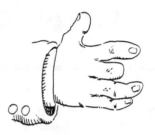

**1**

Close your right fingers together and hold your hand horizontally, palm facing your chest.

**2**

Bend your middle or index finger inward toward your body.

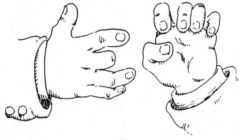

**3**

Bend your left thumb toward your palm.

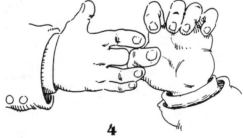

**4**

Now place your thumb next to the bent middle finger.

# *Finger Stretch*

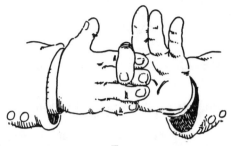

**5**

Next, put your left index finger over
the crack of the two bent fingers.

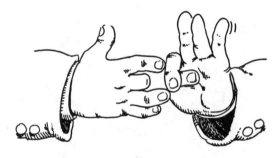

**6**

Finally, move your left hand up and
back. This will give the illusion that your
finger is stretching.

---

Imagine the expressions of awe as your audience notes
the empty space between your knuckle and the
detached finger tip. . .

Not to mention the looks of disgust as they envision the
empty space between your ears.

# 2

# *Two Glasses of Water*

**P**lace bets on this one and pick up a free drink. Stupid? Yes, of course, it's stupid. But people fall for it! Pick a victim who has an I.Q. equivalent to his shoe size, drools constantly and watches Gilligan's Island re-runs on a regular basis. If you stick to these basic requirements, you'll never go wrong.

# *Two Glasses of Water*

**FIRST; the set-up**
Ask the bartender for two cocktail glasses the same size filled to capacity with water, a plate, and three cocktail straws. Put one glass filled with water on top of the plate. The set-up should be done in front of the spectators.

**1**

Place the three cocktail straws across the glass filled with water

# Two Glasses of Water

**2**

Place a cocktail napkin over the second glass filled with water. Try not to let the napkin get wet.

**3**

Place both of your hands palm up around the glass. This will form a cover over the glass.

# *Two Glasses of Water*

**4**

Turn the glass completely upside down and place it on top of the glass with the straws.

**5**

Now quickly pull the napkin completely from the two glasses. The napkin will automatically pull the straws with it. Use your other hand to hold the glasses in place as you're pulling out the napkin.

# *Two Glasses of Water*

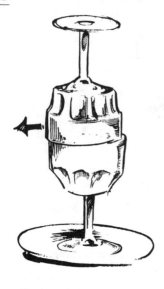

**6**
Push the top glass over about ¼".

Now ask a spectator how much he wants to bet you can make the water in the top glass leave without touching it. Of course they'll say THAT'S IMPOSSIBLE!

**7**
Take one of the straws and blow air in between the two glasses. The water in the top glass will come running out onto the plate, thus proving nothing is impossible.

# 3

# *Cigarette Up the Nose*

Granny used to say, "There are two types of people who are never welcome: moochers and nosey-bodies."

If you're tired of the perennial mooch, the guy or gal who is always asking to "borrow" a cigarette, then this trick is for you.

As Granny said, nobody likes a mooch, but this trick proves that it sometimes pays to be nosey.

# Cigarette Up the Nose

SECRET

No! You don't really put the cigarette up your nose.

Here's how it works:

First you'll need a cigarette, preferably regular size.

**1**

Put your fingers together and hold the end of the cigarette.

**2**

Hold the cigarette up to your nose.

# *Cigarette Up the Nose*

## 3 & 4

Slide your fingers over the cigarette until your fingers touch your nose. This gives the illusion that you have pushed the cigarette up your nose.

## 5

Now hold the tips of your fingers up to your mouth and put the tip of the cigarette in your mouth.

Slide your hand down to reveal the cigarette.

# 4

# *The Power of Love*

**L**ove makes the world go 'round. Faith can move mountains. Prunes can move . . . Oh, forget that one.

. . . But what can the mind do? Is telekinesis (the ability to move objects with the mind) a myth or a reality?

Follow these directions and discover the hidden powers of your own mind.

# *The Power of Love*

**Bar Items Needed:**

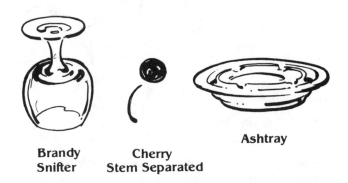

Brandy          Cherry                Ashtray
Snifter      Stem Separated

**Bar Challenge:**

``Keeping the Brandy snifter upside down and parallel
to the bar, move the cherry onto the ashtray without
touching it.''

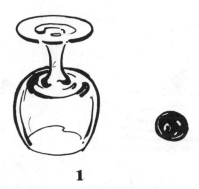

**1**

# *Power of Love*

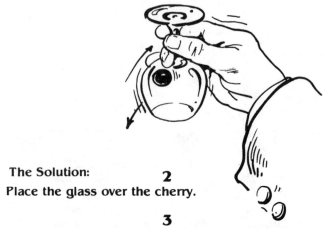

The Solution:      **2**
Place the glass over the cherry.

**3**
Rotate the Brandy Snifter UP and BACK keeping it parallel. Centrifugal force created by the spinning will lift the cherry inside.

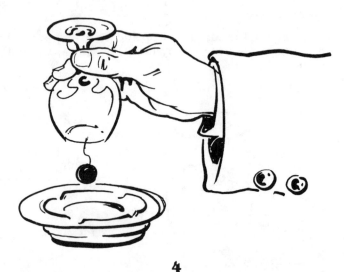

**4**
Quickly, move the glass over the ashtray; the cherry will fall out.

# 5

## *Let There Be Light*

**A** problem that frequently motivates barroom tricksters is how to impress a lovely lady. You know the one we mean; she looks like Greta Garbo, is seated alone and always seems to have a cigarette but no match to light it with.

Believe it or not, all you need to win the eternal admiration of this sultry, sensuous female are the following:

# *Let There Be Light*

This trick requires a small set-up. You need: a rubber band, one safety pin and a pack of matches.

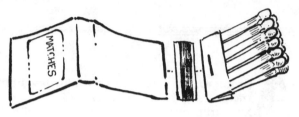

**1**

First rip off the striking part of the match book.

**2**

Fold it in half, striking part in.

**3**

Take a match and put the head in between the folded striking section. Hold the match sandwiched together and wrap a rubber band around it.

Put the safety pin through the top part of the folded striking section and pin it inside your wallet.

# *Let There Be Light*

**4**

To Perform:

Simply open your wallet and pull on the end of the match. It will automatically light.

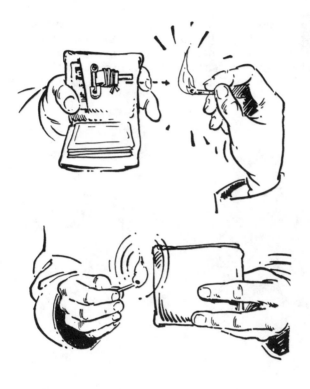

**Warning:** This trick, if successful, can be quite expensive. It seems that pulling a lighted match from one's wallet often leads a woman to assume that your "money is burning a hole in your pocket."

# 6

# *Did You Ever See a Match Burn Twice?*

**I**f you have a tendency toward pyromania and sadism, this is your trick. Strike a match in a nonchalant manner, asking the person next to you, "Have you ever seen a match burn twice?" Blow the match out and "sizzle" the unfortunate victim with the hot end.

**Note:** Along with pyromania and sadism, a tendency to masochism is also helpful, as the final result of this trick is usually a badly bruised trickster.

# 7
## $10 Into $100 Instantly

**H**ere's an idea for making your bar money go further. It lies somewhere beyond the limit of ethics, but just this side of counterfeiting.

# $10 Into $100 Instantly

Here's how to make a ten dollar bill look like $100.

Take a pencil or black pen and draw a line down the center of the zero.

You have just drawn the second zero in your newly created $100 bill.

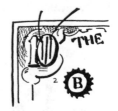

Add more marks on the upper and bottom part of the zeros and you're ready.

Fold the bill and place it under a glass with the $100 sticking out. The dim light inside a bar will make the bill look like the real thing.

So the next time some jerk bets you a hundred dollars you'll be ready. Even if you lose the bet, you'll have only lost ten dollars.

# 8
# *The Stupid Zone*

De da de da
de da de da . . .

**Y**ou're traveling through another bar, a nightclub not only of neon lights and video music, but of mind.

A journey into a flirting world, whose boundaries are that of a casual stare and a wink of the eye.

At the cocktail table up ahead, your next stop; the Stupid Zone.

# The Stupid Zone

**1**

Using a quarter, a nickel and a dime, place them in a row along the table. Pick up a pack of matches and write the word QUARTER on the inside cover. Have one of the girls place her hand over the matches. Say; "This is my prediction."

**2**

Next, borrow a finger ring and direct her friend to; "Look into the ring and think of it as if it were a crystal ball. Now move your hands over the coins in a circular motion from left to right."

(Pause, as she's moving her hands.)

# The Stupid Zone

**3**

"Listen very carefully. Put one hand on one coin and one hand on another."

Notice her hands have covered two coins and one remains in view.

The following will explain how your prediction, the QUARTER, will accurately match her hand movements.

# The Stupid Zone

I.  If the coin she left in view is the _____.

QUARTER, say:  "Our minds are one."
Reveal your hidden answer,
QUARTER, inside the match
cover.

DIME/NICKEL:  Place it in your pocket.

This leaves the QUARTER
and another coin under
each hand.

"Continue looking into the
ring, think carefully, lift one
hand."

II.  If the coin under the hand she raised is the
_____.

QUARTER, say:  "Our minds are one."
Reveal your hidden answer,
QUARTER, inside the match
cover.

DIME/NICKEL:  Place it in your pocket.

The remaining coin under
her hand is now the
QUARTER. Reveal your
hidden answer, QUARTER,
inside the match cover.

# 9
# *Kung Fu Theatre*

**W**atching late night Kung Fu movies on TV might lead one to believe they possess the sacred powers of a black belt. Tell everyone that your skills are far superior to the likes of Bruce Lee and Chuck Norris.

To prove your point explain and perform a trick which no other Karate expert in the world may be capable of doing — SPLITTING FIRE.

# *Kung Fu Theatre*

**1**
Take one plastic cocktail straw and place a match in each end.

**2**
Bend the straw in the center, so the two matches are touching each other.

**3**
Strike another match and light the two matches.

Act like a King Fu expert and give the fire a Karate chop with your other hand.

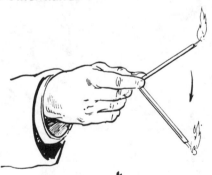

**4**
Slowly, loosen your fingers on the corner of the straw. The plastic will expand and cause the fire to split.

# 10

## Pick a Number

**W**hat is E.S.P.? A sixth sense or just a sophisticated way of second guessing people?

Try this one on a few people and then decide for yourself. Your bewildered spectators will swear you're telepathic.

Open the trick by saying "I learned this one from my old pal, Kreskin." Or "This was a favorite of Albert Einstein."

# Pick a Number

Look at the card below and . . .

## "Pick a number"

$$1\ 2\ 3\ 4$$

Let me see, with my tremendous feats of mind power, the number you picked is three.

How did I do it? Simple.

Since the time you were able to read you've been conditioned to look at words from left to right.

Here's one example:

These three words hold the key to amusing and entertaining privity.

### SKCIRT RABDI PUTS

If you're confused about what these sacred words say, read on.

While the eyes take note of the letters the mind makes no sense of them. The words almost look like a foreign language. But by moving the spaces properly and reading the letters backwards it gives the name of this book, STUPID BAR TRICKS.

Around seventy-five percent of the people will pick three. It's not 100% because there's always some weirdo who has a favorite number which defies all logic.

# Pick a Number

Write the slogan on back of your business card.

Hold it eye level about a foot in front of the person.

Ask them to PICK A NUMBER. Act like you're having a migraine headache, then tell them the number they chose is three.

# *Pick a Number*

They will scream in a frenzy, "Yes." The spectator will no doubt be puzzled how you did this trick.

Hand them this business card with the slogan. They will never lose it; they'll want to try it on their friends to see if they're feeble-minded as well.

Of course they'll say, "Do more; I want to see more."

# 11
---
# *Mentally Remembered*

I f you were pleased by the success of the last trick, and wish to further dazzle your audience, give this one a go.

As with the first "Mentalism" trick, you will be second-guessing your participant.

Perform it properly and the guy next to you will run down the batteries in his pocket calculator before he figures it out.

# Mentally Remembered

Ask a person to: "Think of a two-digit odd number between 1 and 50, like 17, where both of the numbers are odd, not like 22 where they're the same. Think of it and write it down." (Memorize the above statement.)

Repeat the above paragraph again while they're thinking what to write.

Hand them a cocktail napkin to write their prediction. Have them fold it up without you looking at it and hold it between their hands.

Again act like you're having a migraine and write your prediction on another cocktail napkin.

Write 35 on the napkin; then cross it out and write 37. Fold it and hold it next to their napkin.

Ask them to "open their napkin." It will usually say thirty-five or thirty-seven. If they wrote thirty-five, open your napkin and say "I was thinking of thirty-five before I crossed it out." If they wrote thirty-seven, tell them "It's amazing." You wrote thirty-five but for some reason crossed it our and wrote thirty-seven. Either way you can't lose.

# *Mentally Remembered*

How does it work? The power of suggestion.

By telling them to pick a two digit odd number, you have eliminated all the even numbers. And by calling out the numbers 17 and 22 you've pushed them to think of a higher number like 35 or 37.

One similarity of this number trick and the other is there's always some nut with a favorite number who may pick 13, 19 or 39. But if they say 39 you can always tell them how close you were when you predicted 37. So you only have three numbers which can prove you wrong, which means the trick is about 94% accurate.

These two number effects won't make you a professional Mentalist, but they will make you mentally remembered.

# 12

## *How to Hypnotise an Idiot*

**L**et's face it, if you're reading this book in the first place you're probably a power-hungry fiend and downright vengeful to boot. This trick gives you the opportunity to make a complete fool out of some poor slob who is stupid enough to trust you.

# How to Hypnotise an Idiot

## 1

Before performing the trick, hold your beer can above the flame of a cigarette lighter.

You'll notice the bottom part of the can is getting black. Don't touch it. Just place the beer can on the table next to the can without the black stuff. Just remember which is the gimmicked one.

Tell the victim, I mean spectator, that you've taken up hypnotism and you believe they're a suitable subject. Next inform the spectator; "Look into my eyes and do everything I do."

Pick up the beer can *without* the black. Tell them; "Think of the beer can as if it were Aladdin's Lamp."

# *How to Hypnotise an Idiot*

Our model Carolyn, illustrated below, will play the part of the stooge; you play the part of the hypnotist.

**2**

Rub the top of the can. Now they should rub the top of their can. Rub your face. Simultaneously they should be rubbing their face.

**3**

Now rub the bottom of the can. Simultaneously they should rub the bottom of their can.

# How to Hypnotise
## an Idiot

**4**

Now rub your face again. They should rub their face.

**5**

Can you see where this is leading? By putting their hand on the bottom of the can, they'll be placing this black soot all over their face without realizing it.

# How to Hypnotise an Idiot

## 6

Continue this last step until their face is covered with that black junk.

Tell the spectator, "I guess the hypnotism didn't work." After you complete the trick, quickly get up and blend in with the crowd. This is a real crowd pleaser because everyone's in on the gag except for the fool.

# 13
## *Stupid Puzzle #1*

**S**omeone once said that a genius is a person who has learned to "think his way around corners." If you have an inflated opinion of your own intellect, give this a shot *before* you read the solution.

If you have trouble "thinking your way around this corner," don't worry—you'll have the opportunity to stump your friends once you learn the secret.

Problem:  Draw a dot with a circle around it. There may be no lines connecting the dot to the circle and you must not lift the tip of your pen off the paper.

**Well Einstein, giving up so soon?**

# *Stupid Puzzle #1*

Fold the corner of the paper. Draw a dot next to the corner. Now carry your pen over the folded paper, thus enabling you to solve the puzzle.

---

This will probably be performed by the same wiseguy who asks if a match can burn twice.

# 14

## Stupid Puzzle #2

### *Eleven = Nine*

**F**ind a person who claims to be a real brain. Engage him in a conversation concerning the depth of mathematics. If the person begins to mention words like "calculus" he is the perfect choice for this trick.

Ask if he has ever dabbled in theoretical mathematics. Tell him you recently read of an enigmatic equation in which eleven equals nine.

To illustrate the equation, place eleven matches on the bar and ask him to work the problem out.

# Stupid Puzzle #2

How do you turn eleven matches into nine?

   This is yet another subservient puzzle; it is frequently
accompanied by an inane person who thinks he is very
clever. This fools all professors, teachers and
mathematicians because it challenges all logic.

How does it work?

By positioning the matches to spell the word nine.

   You must agree this definitely falls under the
category of Stupid.

# 15

# *The Impromptu Roman Candle*

**A**fter an evening of performing bar tricks, you can create a grand fireworks finale. This pyrotechnical achievement is the result of years of research and many sleepless nights.

**Note:** For an even grander finale, perform this trick over a glass of alcohol. (JUST JOKING.)

# Impromptu Roman Candle

First;

Take two plastic cocktail straws from the bar. Then ask the bartender for a glass of water and a pack of matches or lighter.

To perform;

**1**

Light a match. Now pick up two cocktail straws and hold them together by their ends. Light the ends as if you were lighting a cigarette.

# *Impromptu Roman Candle*

## 2

Blow the match out and hold the lit straw ends about ½ foot over the glass of water. Gently shake the straws.

You'll notice the lit plastic drop into the glass like a mini Roman Candle. After the fire comes close to your fingers, drop the ends into the glass of water.

# 16

# *Volcanic Eruption*

**T**ell your volunteer that you've been studying the effects of geothermal eruptions. Further state that you can generate a volcanic eruption in the palm of his/her hand.

When the volunteer voices disbelief remind him that the laws governing volcanoes are still largely a mystery to us. After all, we were told there were no active volcanoes in North America until Mount St. Helens erupted.

# *Volcanic Eruption*

Before the presentation;

## 1

Secretly stick your fingers in an ash tray to pick up some ashes on the tips of your fingers. One way to conceal this move is by putting a cigarette out in the ash tray.

## 2

Tell a spectator to hold their hand palm face down. Now inform them it's not high enough and lightly touch the tips of your fingers (with the ashes) under the palm of their hand. Simultaneously, move their hand up about a foot higher to conceal this move.

# Volcanic Eruption

Next tell them to close their hand.

So in essence what you've done is put ashes inside a spectator's hand without them realizing it. Explain to them you can make a volcanic eruption take place in their hand.

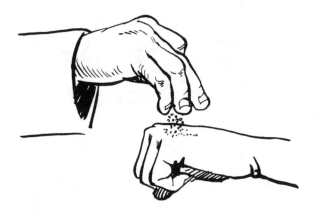

**3**

Sprinkle some ashes over the person's closed hand as if it were salt.

Ask the person if they actually believe an explosion has taken place, an exothermic reaction.

Have the skeptical observer open their hand. Much to their dismay they will have ashes in their hand. Proving once and for all the hand is quicker than the eye.

# 17
# *Famous Coin-in-Ear Trick*

**H**ow would you like to be able to pull money from anyone's ear? Impossible you say? We all know that farmers derive money from ears, but our method is not quite so corny.

# Famous Coin-in-Ear Trick

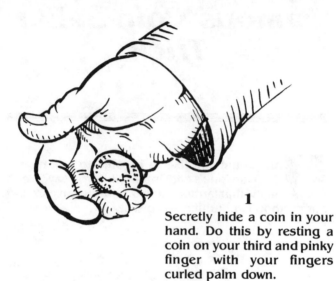

**1**

Secretly hide a coin in your hand. Do this by resting a coin on your third and pinky finger with your fingers curled palm down.

Extend your third and pinky finger holding the coin with your thumb.

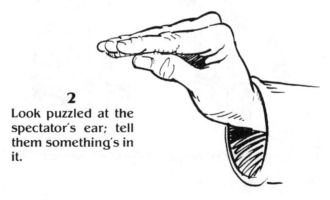

**2**

Look puzzled at the spectator's ear; tell them something's in it.

# *Famous Coin-in-Ear Trick*

**3**
Simply move your finger-
tips by the person's ear
and push the coin halfway
out to display the coin.

After removing the coin, ask the participant if he or she
felt the coin passing through their ear. Naturally they
will answer "no." Then reply that the waxy buildup
inside their ear provided more than adequate
lubrication.

# 18
# *Lone Star Legend*

**M**any moons ago in Lilly's Saloon a legendary
Texas poker bar, a trickster by the name of Dal
the Kid changed the Texas Ten-point star.

He fooled the local cowhands and fleeced them there
that day, by challenging the whole town to all his gold,
fortune and fame.

Not since the likes of Wild Bill Hickock had I ever
observed such a duel. But when the Rainmaker
entered, he just proved the Kid a fool.

# *Lone Star Legend*

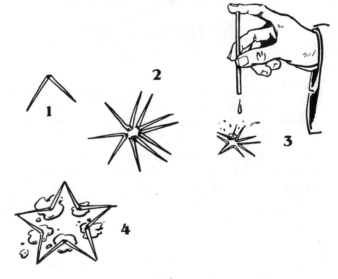

## 1

Take (5) five toothpicks. Break each one in half and form a triangle.

## 2

Now position each of the toothpicks to this pattern.

This is how the Rainmaker turned a ten-point star into five and won the pot of gold.

## 3

Demonstrate the secret by taking a straw and sticking it into a glass of water. Place your index finger on the tip to retain the water.

Now, drop a bit of water on each corner of the triangle.

## 4

Slowly the water will expand the wood toothpicks to form the LONE STAR.

# 19
# *Cutting and Restoring*

**C**utting and restoring is a category which encompasses a great number of tricks. Tricksters since the dawn of time have favored it, creating endless variations.

In American politics we have our own special cutting and restoring game: a Republican president is elected, who quickly sets about cutting budgets. He is followed by a Democrat who miraculously restores all the cancelled expenditures.

# Cutting and Restoring

# A DECAPITATED MATCH

The following trick is a restoration which you can perform anywhere, even without congressional approval.

# A Decapitated Match

Before performing this trick "classic palm" a match.

**1**

To classic palm, place the match in the center of your palm with its ends facing your pinky and thumb, close your hand a little and turn your hand over. Notice how the match stays hidden in your hand.

Now hand a volunteer another match. Tell them to break the match head off its stem - to decapitate the match and hand you both pieces.

# A Decapitated Match

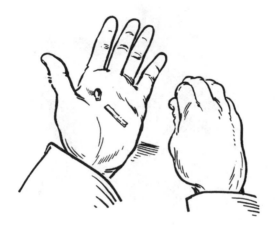

**2**

With your left palm facing up, have them drop the two
pieces into your hand.

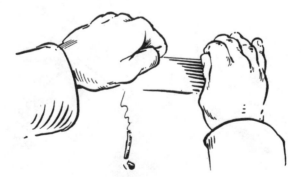

**3**

Close your hand and turn it over. Bring your hand to the
edge of the bar and slightly open your hand and let the
decapitated match pieces drop to the floor.

# *A Decapitated Match*

**4**

Simultaneously, bring your right hand over and press
your two hands together as if you're trying to meld the
match back together.

**5**

Hold your hands in front of the spectator, revealing the
restored match.

# 20
# *Follow the Flame*

I f you happen to run into an old flame at the local
club and you wish to rekindle the acquaintance,
use this little trick as an ice breaker.

# *Follow the Flame*

Borrow a handkerchief from a spectator. Ask two people to hold one end of the handkerchief with each hand, tightly. Take your lighter, flick it so the flame stays on. Rotate it across the handkerchief. If you keep moving the lighter the flame will not burn the handkerchief because the inside of a flame is hollow.

Move the flame off the handkerchief and display their scarf without any holes.

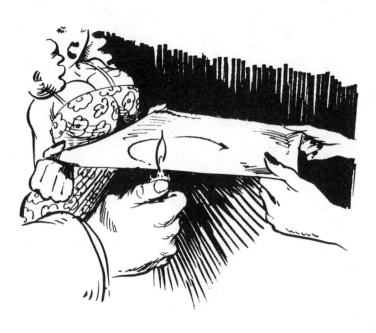

# 21
# *The Bar Spider*

**T**his trick is a particular pleaser where there are ladies present. If you have a date ask her if she is afraid of "creepy, crawly things."

She may reply, "Of course not. If I were, what would I be doing with you?"

Nevertheless, continue undaunted with the performance of the trick. Set the mood by warning people to cover their drinks—a large, alcoholic bar spider has been darting about stealing the patrons' booze.

# The Bar Spider

Effect: a napkin suddenly travels across the bar.

To Begin:

Twist four corners of a cocktail napkin and SECRETLY place a lemon, lime or orange underneath.

Give the fruit a nudge and swiftly the napkin will roll down the bar, creating a crawling spider.

After it travels across the bar, quickly grab the center of the napkin SECRETLY picking up the lemon, lime or orange and drop it on your lap or on the bartender's side of the bar, letting it fall to the floor.

Then show the cocktail napkin is empty.

# 22

## *The Beer Chaser*

**B**arroom buddies are notorious for making little wagers between themselves. You may wish to try this bet on a favorite barroom buddy of yours.

**Warning:** Before pulling this trick on your buddy, make sure he *really is a buddy* - regular practitioners of this trick are often at a loss to explain their black eyes and missing teeth.

# The Beer Chaser

Line up three mugs of beer and have the bettor line up three shot glasses with liquor.

**1**

Tell the spectator:

"I bet you I can drink these three beers before you can drink those three shots of liquor. The only rule is you can't touch my beer mugs."

The sucker will say, "Fair enough."

# *The Beer Chaser*

## 2 & 3

Now begin;

Drink your first beer. Just as the fool is finishing their second shot glass place your empty beer mug upside down over their third filled shot glass. Thus, winning the bet.

# 23

# *The Secret to
a Good Martini*

**A**nyone will tell you the secret to a good martini is
that it should be very dry. So what's the secret?
The method of mixing, of course.

By following these instructions when you are asked to
prepare a martini, you will insure that your patrons will
never complain that it isn't dry enough. Also, you could
save a good deal of money on your liquor bill.

# The Secret to a Good Martini

### 1

Borrow a metal mixing container and a strainer from the bartender. Tell the bartender to fill the container with ice. Ask a spectator what the secret of a good martini is. They should answer a dry martini.

### 2

Fill a shotglass with gin and pour the gin into the mixing container. Put the strainer over the metal mixer and shake. Begin to pour the mixed martini into an empty glass. But nothing comes out; the gin has disappeared.

# The Secret to a Good Martini

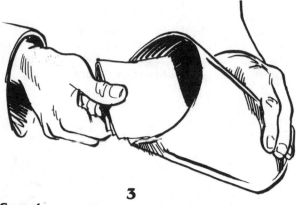

**3**

### The Secret:

Before the ice is put into the container SECRETLY drop three folded cocktail napkins into the metal container. They should drop to the bottom of the can. By shaking the mixer with the ice in it, the liquid is absorbed into the napkins.

ICE

NAPKIN

GIN ABSORBED

# 24

## *The Levitated Glass*

**W**e've all heard about President Clinton's economic theory, "Bubba-nomics". It all sounds great, but somehow the money seems to get caught somewhere in the middle before reaching my hands. This trick is based on sound economic principles.

To illustrate the power of the dollar, display two filled cocktail glasses, a few inches apart. Tell your spectator, "these two glasses represent you and me."

next...

# *The Levitated Glass*

**1**

Then, bring out a dollar bill and a third glass, saying, "This glass represents the Rockefellers of the world, ever held in a position above us by the American dollar. To prove my point and illustrate the strength of a dollar, I'm going to suspend this third glass over the other two with just this one dollar."

Naturally, the spectator will be incredulous, yet interested by your patter. They will say it cannot be done, but at the same time urge you to show them.

# The Levitated Glass

**2**

Fold the dollar bill like an accordion. Now it will sustain the weight of the third glass.

Close by saying, "See, I told you ... The only thing that keeps Rockefeller up there is the almighty buck."

# 25

# *The Fire Lemon*

**W**hen you meet a friend in a bar who is in a bad mood, this trick may help you cheer them up.

Set up the trick by saying, "My, you're in a bad mood. Your disposition is so sour you remind me of a lemon. Of all the fruit in the world, the lemon has the bitterest outlook on life ..."

# *The Fire Lemon*

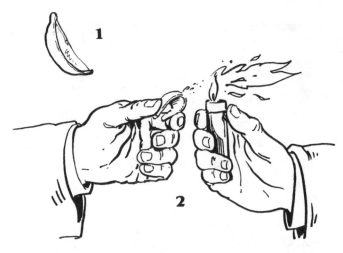

## 1

Take out a lemon slice and show it to them.

Continue, saying, "The old lemon goes around dripping his bitter juice on everyone else and making them miserable, too."

—Peel the lemon—

Put the peel to your lips, taste it, then grimace at the sour flavor ... Now, take out a cigarette lighter.

"But, sooner or later the lemon meets up with a real hot character, like myself, who makes himself a candle in the darkness for everyone he meets. And if that old lemon tries his bitter routine on our friend with the flaming personality ..."

## 2

Squeeze the lemon peel onto the flame of the lighter. A mini-explosion will occur.

". . . the lemon just gets burned out."

This trick is a bit on the sentimental side, but it just may be what's needed to put a smile on your friend's face.

# 26

# *My Palm Line*

**P**ick-up lines are a state of being suave, sophisticated, a sense of *je ne sais quoi*. Glance over
these famous lines;

Would you like to dance?

Can I buy you a drink?

Wanna ride in my '63 Corvette Stingray?

Fellow bar-trickster Dal Sanders uses a sure-fire style.
I'm convinced you'll add this to your own long list. All
you have to do is act like you're reading her palm.

# My Palm Line

After doing a couple of tricks, turn to the young lady sitting next to you and explain that you would like to read her palm. Take her hand and hold it palm up as if you were studying it.

**1**

Lightly rub the palm of her hand. (For some reason women love to have their palms rubbed with a feathery touch.) Pick out a line and tell her; "This is your life line. It looks like a long, interesting one to me."

Then pick another line and explain; "This means you'll have many beautiful clothes. It's called your clothes line." After a moment finish by revealing; "This is your PHONE LINE. If you give me your number, I'll make it RING."

# 27

# *All in the Happy Hour*

**W**elcome to Brio, the newest hottest club in town. As patrons sip on their wine, exchange words of humor · Sam Jasmine the deejay will play your favorite video hits.

I've been waiting, waiting, waiting for a girl like you
I've been hoping, hoping, hoping for my dreams to
    come true.
I still remember the first time I met you
I knew then baby, I could never forget you.
You were the kind of lady I'd always dreamed of
One look was all it took, I was in love . . . .

# *All in the Happy Hour*

Eva? Yes, she's already inside with her friend Jill. I think the two fine ladies are standing by the dance floor.

Follow me, I'll act as your ambassador to the nightlife. First, we'll delight a few with my favorite Stupid Bar Trick ; "Follow the Flame," then our body language takes over.

> You know now baby I can tell the future
> We're going to be together, I hope that suits you
> I can't think of any way for things to be
> Except me with you baby and you with me
> I've been waiting, waiting, waiting for a girl like you
> I've been hoping, hoping, hoping for my dreams to
>     come true.

Relax, enjoy, the next round of drinks are on me. Where at Brio; "the Best of All Possible Happy Hours."